AMAZING OCEAN LIFE

Octopuses

by Colleen Sexton

Kaleidoscope
Minneapolis, MN

Where the Quest for Discovery Begins

Kaleidoscope Publishing, Inc.
6012 Blue Circle Drive
Minnetonka, MN 55343

Library of Congress Control Number
2022937339

ISBN
978-1-64519-561-0 (library bound)
978-1-64519-631-0 (ebook)

Bigfoot Jr. lurks within one of the images in this book. It's up to you to find him!

Table of Contents

Oceans of Octopuses

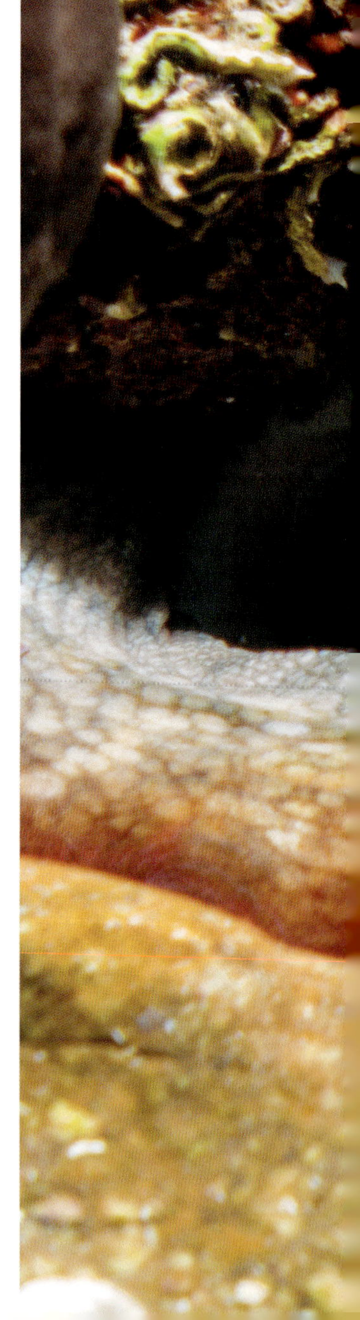

An octopus crawls along the ocean floor. It slips into its rocky **den** to hide.

The octopus is shy. It lives alone.

Octopuses have lived in the oceans for more than 500 million years.

Where Do Octopuses Live?

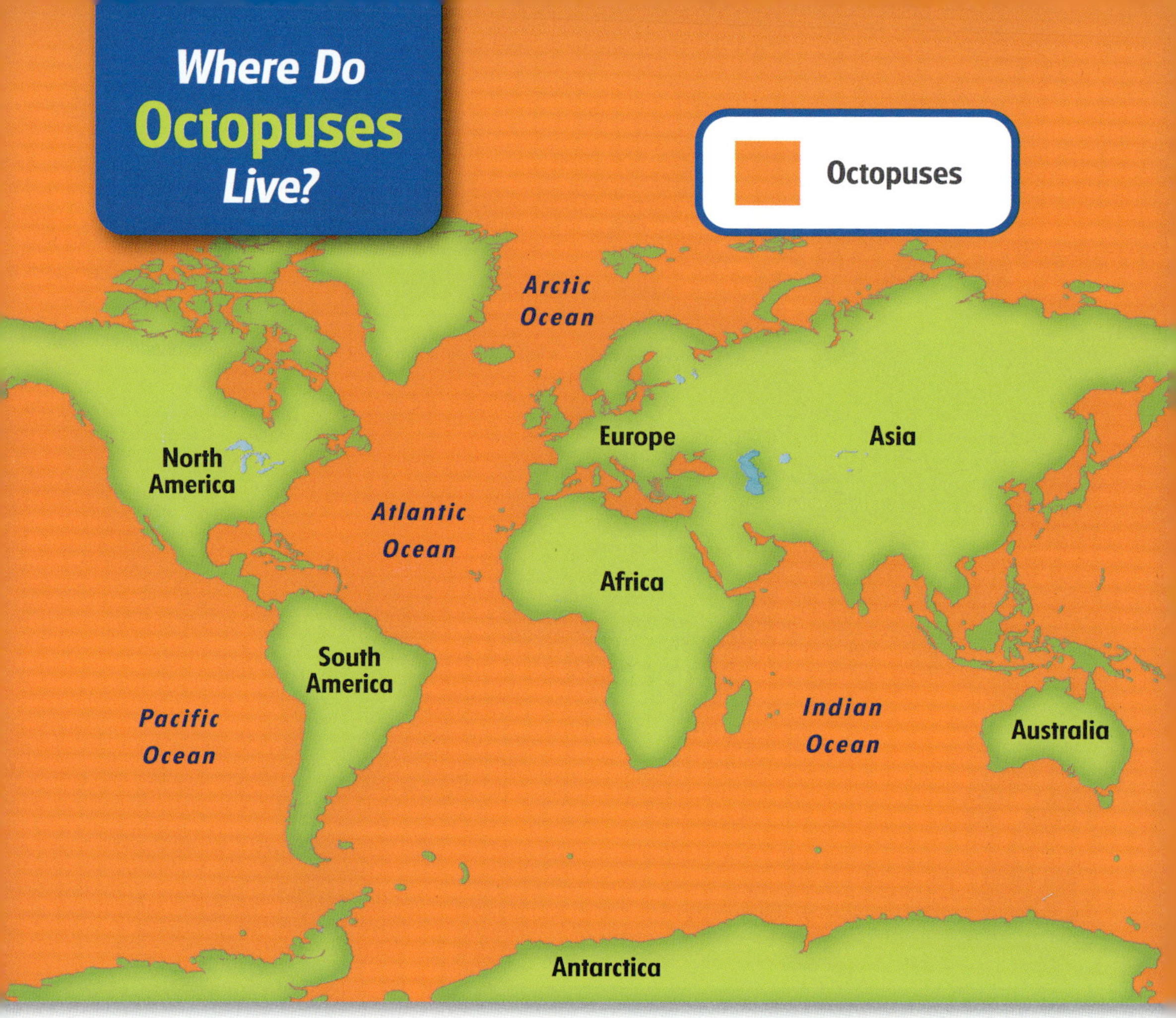

Octopuses

Arctic Ocean
North America
Europe
Asia
Atlantic Ocean
Africa
South America
Pacific Ocean
Indian Ocean
Australia
Antarctica

Octopuses are found in oceans all over the world.

They live in shallow waters near shore. They live deep under the sea.

Soft Bodies

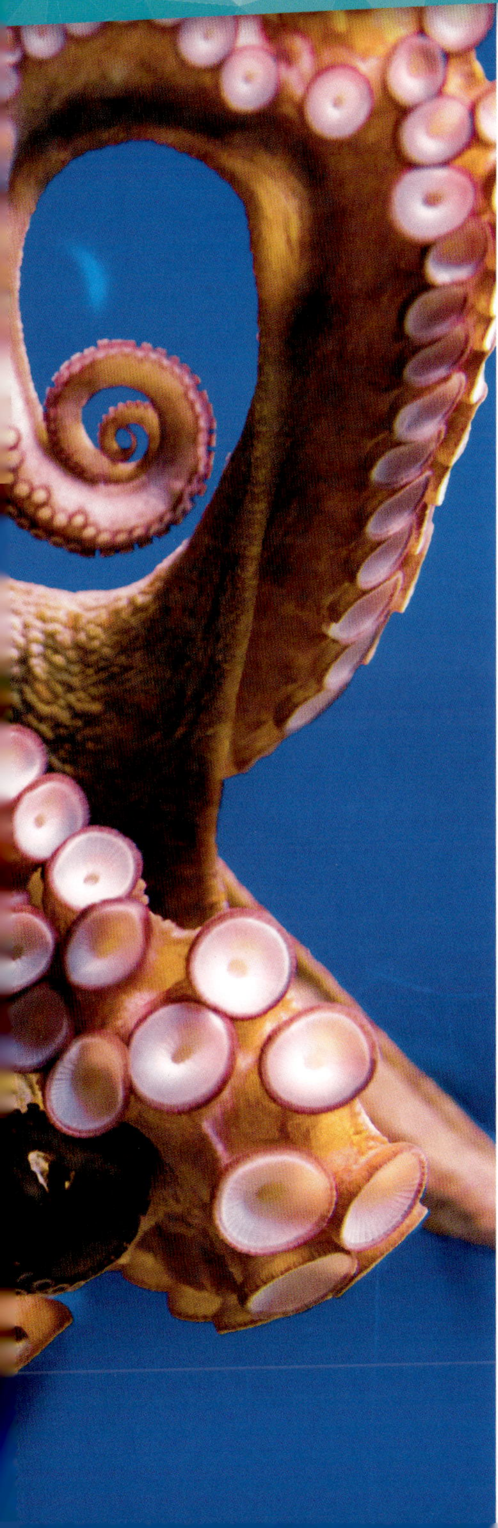

An octopus has a soft, squishy body. It can fit through small spaces.

A **mantle** covers the rounded part of the body. It protects the octopus's **organs**.

FUN FACT
An octopus has three hearts.

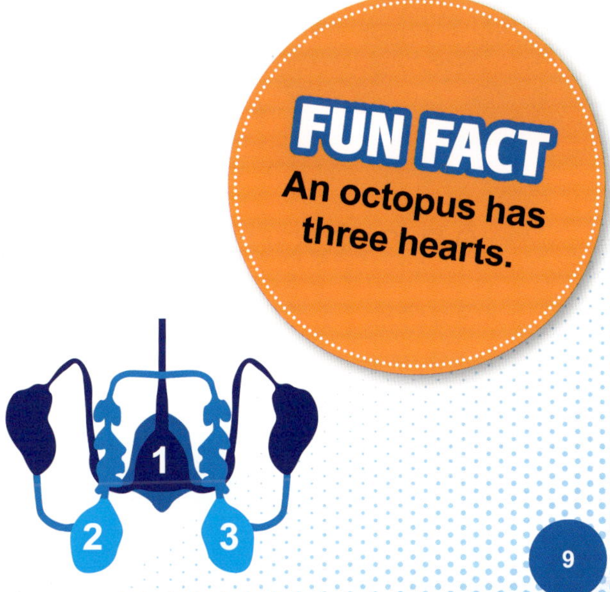

An octopus has huge eyes. They help the octopus see in dark, cloudy water.

An octopus's mouth is in the center of its body. The mouth has a hard **beak**.

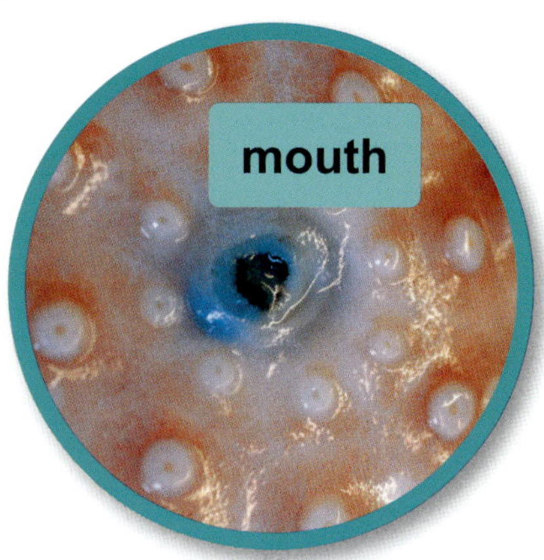

Eight long arms circle the mouth. The arms have **webs** of skin between them.

Each arm has two rows of round **suckers**. They help the octopus crawl.

FUN FACT
An octopus can regrow an arm if it loses one.

Parts of an Octopus

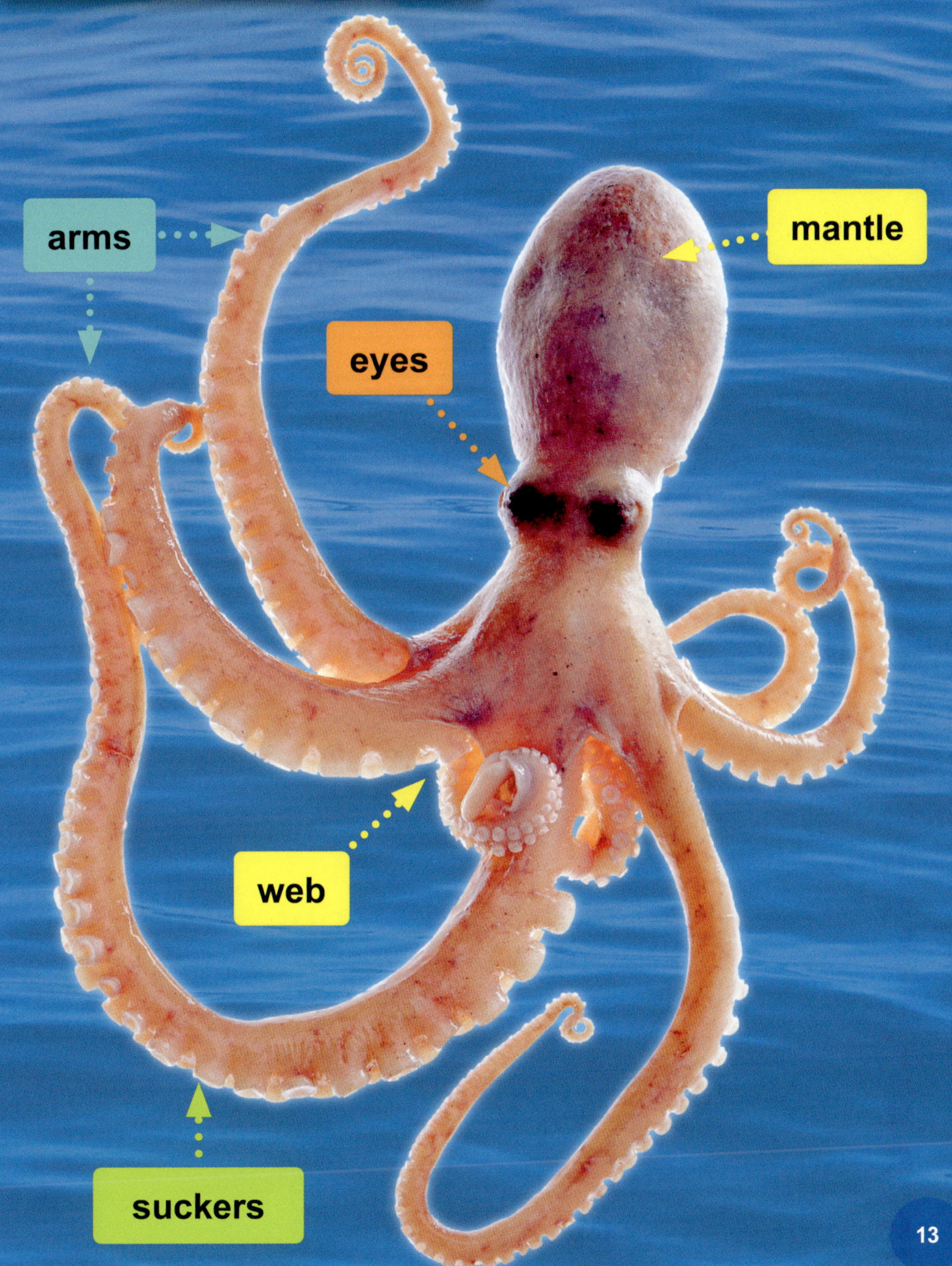

On the Hunt

An octopus hunts at night. It searches for clams, crabs, snails, lobsters, and small fish.

The octopus catches **prey** with its strong arms.

The octopus bites into the prey with its beak. The beak forces poison into the prey.

FUN FACT

Octopuses are some of the smartest animals. Most of their brain cells are in their arms!

Octopuses can smell and taste with their suckers.

The octopus tears apart the prey with its suckers. The arms bring the food to the octopus's mouth.

Escape Artists

When an octopus sees a **predator** come near, the octopus quickly changes its shape and the color of its skin.

The octopus seems to disappear. It matches its surroundings. The octopus fools the predator!

What Eats **Octopuses?**

Octopuses have another way to escape predators. The octopus squirts a cloud of dark **ink** into the water.

The ink cloud surprises the predator. *Whoosh!* The octopus changes color and escapes.

FUN FACT
Octopuses are fast swimmers. They force water through their bodies to speed away.

Photo Glossary

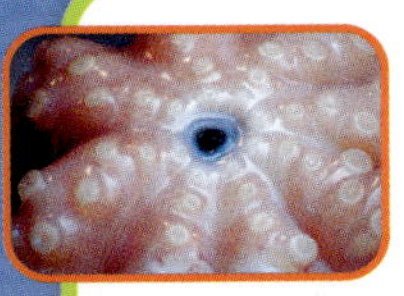

beak: A hard pointed mouth used to bite into food. An octopus has poison in its beak.

den: The home where an animal lives. Octopuses often make their dens between rocks.

ink: A dark liquid that octopuses can squirt from their bodies. An octopus can squirt ink to escape a predator.

mantle: Covers something, hiding it or protecting it. The octopus's mantle helps keep its organs safe.

organs: Inside body parts such as the heart, stomach, and kidneys. The octopus has three heart organs instead of one.

predator: An animal that hunts other animals for food. An octopus can change color and shape to fool its predators.

prey: An animal hunted by another animal for food. An octopus uses its long arms to catch its prey.

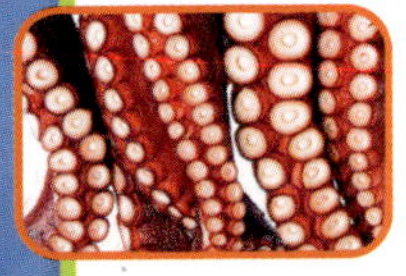

suckers: The round, cup-shaped parts on an octopus's arms. Suckers can bend and stretch to hold onto things.

web: The fold of skin between some animals' toes, fingers, or arms. Octopuses have webbed arms.

Read More

Harris, Bizzy. *Octopuses*. The World of Ocean Animals. Minneapolis, MN: Jump!, 2022.

Montgomery, Sy. *Inky's Amazing Escape: How a Very Smart Octopus Found His Way Home.* New York, NY: Simon & Schuster Books for Young Readers, 2018.

Shaffer, Lindsay. *Octopuses.* Animals of the Coral Reef. Minneapolis, MN: Bellwether Media, 2020.

Factsurfer.com gives you a safe, fun way to find more information.

1. Go to www.factsurfer.com.
2. Enter "Octopuses" into the search box and click 🔍
3. Select your book cover to see a list of related websites.

About the Author

Colleen Sexton is a writer and editor. She is the author of more than one hundred nonfiction books for kids on topics ranging from astronauts to glaciers to elephants. She lives in Minnesota.

INDEX

PHOTO CREDITS

The images in this book are reproduced through Shutterstock: zhengzaishuru 1; pan demin 3, 4, 13; Adam Ke 5; Vladimir Turkenich 6; Tabooma 7; Fotokon 8; Osman Temizel 10; Henner Damke 10, 22; Mila Couto 11; Konstantin Novikov 22; Yellow Cat 12, 17, 22; Ekaterina V. Borisova 14; HP Productions 14; Rich Carey 14, 22, 23; Apisit Chin 14; Shpatak 15; Subhrajit123 16, 22; RayK Photos 18; Vincent Scherer 19; Good luck images 19; Gonzalo Jara 19; Eric Isselee 19; Maria Spb 19; E. O. 19; Vittorio Bruno 20, 22; robertzwinchell 21; lay london 22; Renier Basson 22; Alexey Masliy 22; Jona Sanchez 22. iStock: GeorgePeters 19. Cover: Willyam Bradberry, zhengzaishuru, Solarisys.